GOTD

GREJ OF THE DAY

Knowledge is cool!

15 AMAZING STEP-BY-STEP MICRO LESSONS

Micael Hermansson

BIGBUSINESS PUBLISHERS

ⓒ Colofon

Original title: Grej of the Day – Lust för kunskap, Sweden 2018
Dutch adaptation: Grej of the Day – Kennis is cool!, The Nether-
lands, 2019
English translation: Philippa Burton, 2020
Cover design: Miranda de Groot, Twin Media bv
Inside design: Marta Coronel, Studentlitteratur
Inside layout: Twin Media bv
Publisher: Donald Suidman, BigBusinessPublishers

 Facebook: Grej of the Day (International)
www.grejoftheday.com

ISBN 9789493171152

Contents

Wow!

For the past ten years I have started most school days with Grej of the Day (GOTD). These micro lessons last eight to ten minutes and set the tone for the rest of the day. The interesting and exciting topics of GOTD are meant to inspire and arouse curiosity.

The Grej of the Day method is used throughout Scandinavia. It is also growing popularity in the Netherlands and Belgium, and beyond the borders of Europe. You can apply it to all ages and in all classes of primary school, secondary school, special education and adult education. Teachers exchange their own *grejs* in Facebook groups and on various websites.

Everyone can work with GOTD. This method fits into all lesson plans and they are fun! Whether you already use Grej of the Day, or are hearing about it for the first time, this book explains the method and how to achieve maximum impact: Students who say *Wow!* in class.

I hope you get a lot out of this book.

Micael Hermansson
Umeå / Tärnaby, March 2020

Micael worked as a teacher for thirty years (1986-2015). 2009 he started exploring the power of micro lessons and soon GOTD started spreading.
In 2015 Micael received the title "Best teacher in Sweden" and in 2019 "Best public speaker in Sweden".
The last six years Micael has been working fulltime as an author - writing e.g. six GOTD-books - and as an international keynote speaker, including TEDtalks.

What will you find in this book?

The word "grej" means "one thing" in Swedish. Grej of the Day – also known by its abbreviation GOTD – is quite simply 'thing of the day'. It is an inspiring micro lesson based on a specific approach. I have chosen to call this concept Grej of the Day, or GOTD, in English as well.

This book is made up of four short parts.

1. Background

I explain how Grej of the Day came about and developed.

2. What is GOTD?

I tell you what characterizes GOTD. In a nutshell: You send children home with a clue about tomorrow's *grej*. The following day, you give them the eight to ten minutes long micro lesson, you discuss it together with your students and you give them the next clue.
In this section of the book, I share my experience regarding the impact of GOTD on students.

3. Working with the GOTD model

Here you find the step-by-step model that I believe provides the fastest and most efficient approach and best results.
–   What to take into account during the preparations and planning
–   What to do during the micro lesson itself
–   How to extend the lesson with follow-up questions
–   How students can work with the material

... and finally some valuable tips

4. The micro lessons

Every Grej of the Day lesson is clearly presented on two pages. Here you find everything you need before, during and after the micro lesson. All the GOTDs in this book have the same build-up:

1. On the left-hand side, a summary of important facts with a clue.

2. On the right-hand side, alternative clues, facts, particulars, questions and tips for further topics.
   This book includes a step-by-step manual for working with Grej of the Day and 15 sample lessons.

1 Background

The idea for Grej of the Day came to me one day in 2009, totally out of the blue. It was indeed at one of those moments when I needed it most.

I had been in the profession for quite some time (twenty-five years) and had already had a number of more or less successful ideas to increase student involvement and maximize the transfer of knowledge. I had been struggling for a while with how to reach out to the entire class in the best way possible. I wanted all the students to be enthusiastic, not just a few!

It was frustrating. No matter what method I tried, there were always a significant number of students who could not answer the simple question 'What did you learn today?' Instead they answered "Nothing special". This was painful to hear.

The first grej

In autumn 2009 I had a new class and decided to try out my brand new idea. I remember my first GOTD very well. The students came in. I had written a question on the black board: "Why don't polar bears eat penguins?"

My students started the day with 20 minutes of independent reading, and I saw many of them peeking at my question wondering about it, instead of reading their books. I explained that we were trying out a new idea, called Grej of the Day. Every morning I would tell them something new and interesting and I wanted them to keep notes in a special GOTD notebook.

The students were not overly enthusiastic, but I pushed ahead with it.

The answer to the question was that the polar bears live at the North Pole and the penguins live at the South Pole. This answer led me to our first GOTD-topic: The South Pole. I showed a few photographs, pulled out a map, spoke about low temperature records, thickness of ice and gave an abbreviated version of the race to the South Pole involving Roald Amundsen and Robert Falcon Scott. I had finished in less than nine minutes.

To my great surprise and joy, the students were fascinated. They listened attentively and took in the information. When I had finished, they had so many questions and thoughts. The best part was how they cheered when I announced that Grej of the Day was to become our new morning routine. They really liked the idea. I wrote a new clue on the board for the following day and felt that this might be the beginning of something very exciting.

More than ten years later, I am still not exactly sure what happened. The micro lessons were all my pupils ever spoke about. They rushed up to me in the schoolyard with their answers to yesterday's clue, and went home in the afternoon with a burning desire to show and tell their families what they had heard and learnt at school. 'Dad, we spoke about cheetahs today. Did you know that...' or "Mum, have you heard of Marie Curie?"

A couple of weeks later I put up a sign in our classroom with a slogan that was to become our motto: "Knowledge is cool".

Unexpected impact

The impact of the micro lessons exceeded all my prior successes. The reactions and enthusiasm of students were truly exceptional. In just a few weeks' time I noticed that the children not only loved this new routine in the morning, but also started dealing with school differently. They had become curious and some took school more seriously. They also appeared happier. The students were proud of their newly acquired knowledge, something I had never seen before. I also noticed another positive impact: Class cohesion increased because this new 'thing' belonged to all of us.

I enthusiastically told colleagues and friends about Grej of the Day and the positive reactions of students, but I guess it sounded too good to be true. No one really believed me and no one tried it out for themselves. Four years later a colleague tried GOTD with great success and then it spread from colleague to colleague. GOTD started spreading fast.

Personally, I knew and felt from the start that GOTD was something special. I saw students who had never given much attention to school suddenly making their own GOTDs in order to surprise their parents and me. I noticed how incredibly motivated they became and how they loved this concept:

1. The clue - get them exciting the day before.

2. The micro lesson - keep it short.

3. End the lesson with a "WOW" to increase the curiosity and interest in the subject.

4. Retell from heart at home - the students would blow their partents' minds with amazing facts.

Still, I did not realize at the time, November 2009, that the idea would spread outside Sweden, all over the world.

What is GOTD?

What is Grej of the Day? I will give you my own description and that of my students.

My own description: Grej of the Day is a WOW-fact micro lesson that lasts eight to ten minutes and that I generally give every day - hence its name. I switch randomly between three categories: *people*, *places* and *events/other* of importance that have somehow changed the world, or have had an influence on it. A *grej* is a short stand-alone story that is told succinctly. Over the long term, you start to notice how you can tie together knowledge from different domains. After a while you can see a world wide web of knowledge growing infront of your eyes.

My student's description: Grej of the Day are super short lessons that we get nearly every morning. Micael comes up with an interesting or unusual topic, usually something we know little or nothing about. He tells us a short fairytail of facts, and we listen and take notes in our GOTD notebooks. We usually have many questions or comments afterwards. Micael often uses pictures with a few key words, and complements these with additional info that is particularly fun to know. We are always asked to tell about today's GOTD from heart at home, so we will remember it better. All of our GOTD's are gathered on a big "GOTD-wall" - a world map surrounded by pictures of all the "grejs". The "grejs" are pinpointed on the word map with a thread.

What is the impact of GOTD?

When I started doing this in 2009, I wanted to share all sorts of interesting and inspiring knowledge so the students would become acquainted with new and exciting domains. My mission was to guide them and to point out the interesting things that would tickle their curiosity and stir their imagination. From now on they would want to know as much as their teacher!

However, after a while I noticed that this approach had far more to offer:

* We developed a fun morning routine. Every day had a clear beginning. My students learnt something new and exciting first thing every morning and therefore felt empowered by knowledge.

* My students knew all sorts of interesting facts about just about everything: from Cleopatra to Yuri Gagarin to tsunamis and the atomic bomb.

But the gains went far beyond these two aspects. GOTD turned out to have side effects that were more important still.

Everybody participates

I soon noticed that all students tended to become involved in these lessons, rather than just the talented and high performing few. It is even possible that less interested and weaker students were those who benefitted most. How could this be? Was it the short and fast presentation? Or the repetitive character of the working model? Were they finally getting the feeling of having learnt something useful or new?

Stimulating follow-up questions

The micro lessons always elicited other exciting follow-up questions and thought experiments in both the students and myself. 'Why did she think that?' 'What if he had done this instead of that?' 'What similarities and differences do you see between...?'

There were always new opportunities to analyse, imagine, discuss and debate.

Teasers and cliffhangers

I soon realised that it was smart to work with both teasers (tantalizing advance information like clues that make you "prethink") and cliffhangers (sometimes stopping halfway through something exciting to keep the interest alive). During a GOTD I would sometimes take the opportunity to "introduce" topics that we would work with later. This early "sowing technique" proved useful. Students were

9

curious and interested. When we finally got to work on a topic, they had already acquired a lot of information on it, and we did not have to start from scratch. Prior knowledge makes it easier to learn new things. For example, my class of 11-year-olds wanted to do a space assigment. We discovered that they already knew a lot thanks to GOTD. We had done the *grej* on Apollo 11, and lessons on Neil Armstrong and Apollo 13 ('Houston, we have a problem'). The asteroid belt was familiar, as were Laika and Valentina Tereshkova. We had also studied the planets.

We knew that Pluto no longer counted as a planet, what caused the ebb and flow and we had also discussed comets. It was fantastic to be able to recall these items rapidly. Everyone had the feeling that new aspects of space did not have to be that complicated.

Pertinent links

Most interesting by far is how we started to discern patterns and connections over time – after we had done about 20-25 GOTDs.

For instance:

- Napoleon's name popped up both during the GOTD on the Rosetta Stone and when we wondered why the Bernadotte family sits on the Swedish throne.

From Marie Curie to Albert Einstein, and beyond to the atomic bomb, or from Curie to another Nobel Prize laureate, Mother Teresa, a symbol of charity like the Dalai Lama.

- We discovered that Jesse Owens, Rosa Parks and Nelson Mandela were all connected to the struggle for equal rights, but also that Rosa Parks was a great source of inspiration for Martin Luther King.
- The Olympic Games in Berlin in 1936 are connected with the Berlin Wall, but also with Hitler and the ancient Olympics (and of course so did Jesse Owens again).
- The world's largest diamond – Cullinan – was found in South Africa and turned out to have inspired the famous Finnish board game 'The Lost Diamond'.

As you see, there are endless possibilities for connecting knowledge in various fields, which greatly contributes to the efficacy of GOTD. The challenge is to start seeing connections everywhere. Do not hesitate to stop the lesson and ask: 'Do you remember when we talked about...?' Soon the students will also discover these connections themselves.

Scientific evidence

Although I did not realize it at the time, my recipe included a number of ingredients that scientific research has identified as solid learning approaches.

One of the most effective is the short duration of the lesson. We know that we have a limited attention span, but nearly everyone, including children, can manage eight minutes without losing focus.

The 'Zeigarnik effect' provided evidence for the powerful effect of clues and riddles. Psychologist Bluma Zeigarnik (1900-1988) showed how we remember unfinished tasks better than tasks we have completed. Her supervisor, the well-known psychologist Kurt Lewin, got the idea on a busy terrace in Berlin. Waiters knew exactly who had ordered what, but after people had paid, they forgot. The Grej of the Day clue is one of these unfinished tasks. It lights up the brain and makes you curious. My super-short micro lessons were NOT supposed to tell everything - they were used to inspire and create interest.

My insistence on students repeating at home what had interested them during the lesson turned out to be an effective method for memorizing facts. In the psychology of learning it is called the retrieval or testing effect. If at the end of the day you ask students to repeat what they have learnt, they will remember these items better. This can be further strengthened with a weekly, fun quiz on all the "grejs" you have done, for example.

Over the years I noticed that students spontaneously practise different skills when we work with GOTD – from learning new concepts and making connections, to spotting similarities and differences, to structuring information, and seeing topics from different points of view.

GOTD: Step-by-step

I hope you are inspired and ready to begin with GOTD! I am sure that Grej of the Day presents fantastic possibilities for learning new knowledge and practising various skills. Now I will explain my step-by-step plan.(I only wish I had lined it up so neatly for myself when I started).

Preparation and planning

Before giving a micro lesson, do the following:

1. Select a topic

Select a GOTD topic the day before or perhaps earlier.

- Keep it short and well circumscribed

Select a topic with a clear storyline. E.g.: 1. Penguins are birds that can swim very well but not fly. 2. There are many types of penguins. 3. The most famous are emperor penguins that have to work very hard to care for their chicks. Some teachers choose topics that are very broad indeed, like 'the prehistoric period', or 'China'. With broad topics you inevitably end up telling a bit of this and a bit of that, without head or tail, or a clear *Wow!* moment. If you instead choose and zoom in on Dinosaurs, or the Great Wall of China, you will have more than enough material to select from.

- Zoom out

When you zoom in on a 'small' topic, you keep it circumscribed. During the lesson you should indeed zoom out briefly, to situate the topic in a broader context. You can easily relate the Great Wall of China to the history of China, but also to wars, refugees, the Berlin Wall or the United Nations. Such connections stimulate pupils for further *grejs*.

- Go forthe magic WOW!

A *grej* is not a traditional presentation. In a traditional presentation you explain that a guinea pig is a mammal, what they eat, their gestation time, and how to take care of them. A bit of this and a bit of that. Whereas a *grej* on guinea pigs zooms in on a *Wow!* factor, like the different sounds that guinea pigs use to communicate or that their teeth continue to grow throughout their lives. I always used the wow-factor to keep their interest (and always saved the best for last).

- Select a topic that interests you

If you are enthusiastic, students will sense this, and your enthusiasm will be catching. You should not shy away from topics you find challenging. Show your own amazement at what you have learnt while preparing for the *grej*.

- Start with a few of mine

Making your own grejs is a lot of fun, but I do advise practising with a few from this book first. This will give you a feeling for well circumscribed topics, for zooming in and out, for Wow! facts and realizing what happens when you keep your "lessons" really short.

- Alternate

When you go from one theme to another, you get the element of surprise. An animal, a historical person, a natural phenomenon and so forth – make sure you alternate and pick topics randomly. Think of it as pieces of a puzzle. At first it is just one amazing fact here and one amazing fact there... but after a while they can se the big picture.

2. Present the clue

Give the students a clue on the day preceding the micro lesson. Write the clue on the board before they go home (and post it on the class's website, or give it to them on a piece of paper, for instance). This stimulates the curiosity of the students. At home, they may search online for the answer or ask family members. You all agree that the students should keep the answer to themselves. Everyone must have the opportunity to think about it quietly and to search on their own.

This book presents a clue and a couple of alternate clues for every topic. Naturally, you can also come up with a clue yourself.

Tips for the clues

* Make sure the clue is well suited to the age of the group.
* The clue should not be too difficult, in order not to discourage students. This is not a competition but a clue that is too easy, isn't fun.
* Factual clues are easy to come up with and fun to search for: the world's largest animal, the first woman to fly across the Atlantic, etc.
* Quotes are exciting. For instance, 'The eagle has landed.'
* Use a photograph or part of a photograph, like the claw of an animal, a blurry portrait or part of a jigsaw puzzle.
* Sounds can also be great fun.
* Provide a more difficult clue in the morning and before they go home ask students if anyone wants a second, easier clue.
* Clues may be hidden. Give pupils various short assignments throughout the day, so they can gradually guess the clue they will be taking home that evening. You can make this as fun as you want.

3. Read up on the facts

To ensure a micro lesson goes as easily and smoothly as possible, the book presents a compact explanation of the topic with an overview of pertinent facts. It is important that you read up on the topic. Students will soon realise whether you are knowledgeable on the topic or not. Naturally, you do not need to know everything about it. The essential information can be found in many places, such as internet, school books, professional magazines, TV programmes and newspapers.

Jot down a few keywords and keep the text at hand, if necessary. When you prepare for the lesson, try to estimate how long it will take. If possible, you can immediately make connections with current news items or earlier micro lessons. You can also give students the assignment to read further about current developments on that specific topic.

4. Make your slideshow

Make your own slideshow. The slideshow presentation should include:
1. The clue
2. Basic facts (what, when, where) Use only keywords. It is important to add a large image.
3. Other interesting facts that need to be told – one fact per slide. Use as few written words as possible. Avoid full sentences and add a big picture.
3. Exceptional facts (the *Wow!* factor) with an image.
4. Potential questions

You can add as much information or as many images or short films as you want. But my best tip is: Keep it short and simple. This is supposed to be ONE interesting piece - NOT the complete puzzle.

Keep it simple

Over the years, I have discovered that it works better if you keep it simple. My tips:

Tell a story - a fairytale of facts. Make sure the students are listening rather than trying to read sentences on your slides.

Ask yourself what the main point of the story is. Which fact, development or question should linger in the mind of your audience?

For instance:

Alfred Nobel discovered dynamite, became wealthy but expressed regret.

The Eiffel Tower is impressive, but with 25,000 visitors per day, it might not be a very relaxed outing.

Mother Teresa dedicated her life to the poor. What makes that so special?

Build your story and slides in such a manner that the key to the story becomes crystal clear. For Alfred Nobel you will naturally need a minimum of three slides: the invention, success and regret (which led to the Nobel Prizes).

Exclude anything that does not contribute to this key message.

Let the slideshow support your story with nothing more than the keywords and images. One great "TED talk rule" I try to follow is the 10-40 rule: That means that on 10 slides should not be more than a total of 40 words.

You can do a lot of fun things with a slideshow. But make sure your slideshows do not distract. So again, keep it simple:
- no busy or flashy background
- tone down the font usage
- one good image at a time
- if you want more than one image, use additional slides

Use a presenter, one of those handheld clicking devices with which you switch slides without having to walk over to the laptop or look up at the screen, so you can continue to look at your audience.

14

Prepare the students

1. Motivate students to do two things: search for the answer to the new clue at home with their parents. They are also supposed to tell their parents about the micro lesson they just had.

2. Teach students to jot down a few important words or sentences, preferably in a special Grej of the Day notebook. Make sure they keep it short. They do not have to write entire sentences. This to avoid unnecessary frustration.
Tip: If the children have trouble making notes, discuss these difficulties with them afterward. Write down on the board a few of the words mentioned by students so everyone can copy these. If this is still too difficult, you can put a few keywords or short sentences on paper, print this out for the children and have them glue it in their notebooks. This is also part of the micro lesson, although the main emphasis should be on you telling a fairytale of facts and the children listening.

The micro lesson, step by step

I use my micro lessons as day openers. Grej of the Day provides a positive and exciting beginning to the day and even encourages students to arrive on time. It is also a perfect item on which to close the day, or to use as an intermezzo if you notice that attention is lagging during a mathematics lesson, for instance. Try doing one every day for a week, to see the effect it has on the involvement of students. I generally do one every day, but you may prefer one or two per week. Important note: One per week equals about 35 GOTD per school year. One per day equals about 180... That's a big difference.

1. Preparations

* Ask students to get their GOTD notebook, pencil and eraser, and colouring pencils if necessary. Show the students the first slide of your slideshow, the one with the clue. They should write down the clue and date in their notebooks.

* Ask the students about their conversations at home regarding the previous "grej". Did they come across anything they could connect to the previous *grej*? For instance: 'Yesterday I saw a girl on TV who was travelling in India. There was the Taj Mahal!'

2. Solve the clue

* Let the children guess the topic of today's GOTD.

* Listen carefully to the students, to understand the directions in which they searched.

* Afterward, show the topic on the board. The students can write down the topic in their notebooks

3. Present the facts

* Begin the micro lesson. Show the students the second slide, the one with the "what?", the "when?" and the "where?". Begin telling your fairytail of facts. Tell your students the story of your chosen topic. Inspire them with your enthusiasm. Let your students look at the pictures in your slideshow while you are talking about facts related to them.

* The micro lesson must be short and intense: eight to ten minutes. Do not go beyond this time period, or you will significantly diminish its effect.

* The children should not ask questions while you are telling the story. They have the opportunity to do so afterward.

* Sometimes a micro lesson is so incredibly interesting that it develops into something larger. If the children are particularly curious about a topic, you may choose to go into it more deeply some other time. This is something which you as the teacher are best able to judge.

4. Note-taking and drawing

* You can influence how the children take notes. Grej of the Day focuses on listening, so do not ask the children to write down too many things.

* I use notebooks. On the left-hand page the students write the topic, together with the clue, the lesson number and the date. Underneath they have half a page to draw. On the right-hand page I let them take short notes.

* It is up to you whether you let children take notes while they are listening to the story, or afterward. It is probably good to have them write a few keywords, or a short opinion.

* For younger students you can prepare 'fact sheets' that they can glue in their notebooks after the lesson.

* Sometimes it is useful to give the children an image to glue in their notebook.

5. Answering questions

* After you have told the story, you can ask a few questions (also put these in your slideshow). These can include 'do you remember' questions, and questions asking for an opinion. These questions can also be used the next school day as a follow-up.

* After you have given a few micro lessons you may also decide to quiz the children on these.

* At the end of each lesson, give the pupils three minutes to make a drawing and organize their notes. Or they may choose to finish a previous GOTD.

16

6. Home assignments and the clue for the following GOTD

∗ Give the students the clue for the following *grej*. Remind them not to share their answers and thoughts with their classmates, to give everyone the opportunity to think and guess for themselves.

∗ Their home assignment is to briefly retell from heart to their families the topic of the *grej* that was discussed in class. If you are planning on doing another micro lesson the following day, they should also discuss the clue for that at home.

∗ At the end of the school day you can give the children a few minutes to think about or tell a classmate what they are going to retell home.

∗ The GOTD wall: Print an image of every *grej* and hang it close to a map of the world (or of your country or continent). Then run a thread from that image to the place on the map. This has been a very appreciated part of GOTD and everywhere I travel I see classrooms with marvelous and colorful GOTD walls.

∗ With this map the Grej of the Day method receives plenty of attention. It is a concrete way of visulazing what and how much they have learnt. They often stand in front of the GOTD wall, just admiring it and having conversations with each other about all the amazing facts.

7. Create links to other topics

Once you have completed a number of GOTDs, you can point to connections between the different *grejs*, as well as with other events. The Statue of Liberty was built by the same person who designed and built the Eiffel Tower: Gustave Eiffel. Or: 'Yesterday, I saw a TV programme on an aviator, Amalia Earhart.' In such cases, you can easily show the physical connections on your world map.

8. Exchange experiences and GOTDs with other enthusiastic teachers.

For this, please consult the Facebook group **Grej of the Day (international)**. You can adapt the *grejs* of colleagues, to make them suitable for the level you are teaching. Please note: Use big pictures and only a few keyword in the slideshows and avoid a profusion of images, letter types and other distracting elements. Always end your presentation with amazing *Wow! facts*

Final tips before you begin

Now you are ready to begin. I still have a few golden tips to ensure that working with GOTD goes as smoothly as possible.

* Read up on your topic. The students will notice immediately if you only know what is mentioned on your slideshow. Spend a good fifteen to twenty minutes familiarizing yourself with the topic. Study it on the left-hand page in this book. It pays off!

* I know it is tempting, but do not let students choose the topics for you. I used to do this at first, but one of the important points is to open up new vistas for them onto yet unknown and exciting facts. This is why I will sooner choose a *grej* on the Dalai Lama than one on Justin Bieber.

* My motto is: 'Knowledge is cool!' And I would like to add: 'Knowledge should be fun!'

* Do not forget to vary! Surprise your students and yourself. Dare to learn from things that did not work very well.

* The joy and energy you spread with Grej of the Day – as with all of your lessons – make a big difference, both to you and your students. Now that is a fun fact! And a promise.

Remember:
- GOTD is a micro lesson - not a 45 minute lesson with a clue.
- A lot of teachers give only one "grej" a week... That is a good start for sure, but try two or three a week and see what happens!
- Last but not least: It is pretty easy to pick famous men as a topic. Please be careful and make sure that at least 50% of the persons you pick are women.

Let's begin!

4 **Fifteen micro lessons**

Contents

Anne Frank

The Netherlands was occupied by the Germans during the Second World War. The Jewish Anne Frank went into hiding from the Nazis in 1942. She kept a diary during the period she was in hiding. The diary received world fame following Anne's death.

Anne Frank was born on 12 June 1929 in Frankfurt am Main in Germany. There was little work and much poverty in Germany and the country's leader Adolf Hitler blamed Jews for these problems. To escape Hitler's Nazis, Anne Frank's family moved to Amsterdam, the Netherlands in July 1933. The family consisted of her father Otto, her mother Edith and her older sister Margot. In 1941, Anne switched from primary school to the Jewish Lyceum. Jewish children were no longer allowed to attend non-Jewish schools.

Life became increasingly difficult for Jews in Europe. They were banned from parks, cinemas and shops. Anne's father was forced to give up his company. When her sister was summoned up to go and work in Germany in 1942 her parents were alarmed an decided to hide to escape persecution.

The company of Anne's father was situated at 263 Prinsengracht in Amsterdam where he prepared a hiding place in a Secret Annex. The door between the front of the house and the Secret Annex was hidden by a bookcase. Other people were also hiding in the building. Anne and her family lived there for two years.

Anne kept a diary during the years she lived in the Secret Annex. She wrote about every-day events, but also her ambition of becoming a writer. After more than two years the family was discovered. In August 1944 they were transported, first to Westerbork in the Netherlands, and from there, onto the Auschwitz-Birkenau concentration camp.

On 28 October 1944, 1,308 women left Birkenau for the Bergen-Belsen concentration camp, including Anne and her sister. Their mother stayed behind and died on 6 January 1945. It is not entirely clear when Anne and her sister passed away, but it was probably in February or March 1945, from typhus.

Anne's father Otto was the only family member to survive the horrors of the concentration camps. He came into possession of Anne's diary which made a deep impression on him. Otto edited his daughter's diary and *The Diary of a Young Girl* was published in Dutch on 25 June 1947. The book was later translated into approximately 70 languages. Anne's father hoped that readers of the diary would become aware of the dangers brought about by a hatred of Jews, discrimination and racism. Anne Frank's paper archive also includes her *Book of Beautiful Sentences*, in which she recorded loose sentences and passages from books she read in the Secret Annex.

The Anne Frank House is a museum and monument to the memory of Anne Frank and her Jewish family. It receives nearly one million visitors per year.

wikipedia.org., annefrank.org

ALTERNATIVE CLUES

* This young girl never knew she would become world famous
* The writer of *The Diary of a Young Girl*

FACTS

* Born 12 June 1929 in Frankfurt am Main
* Of Jewish origin
* The persecution of Jews
* Lived in Amsterdam In hiding in a Secret Annex
* Wrote a diary
* Died in 1945 In the Bergen-Belsen concentration camp
* Her diary was translated into approximately 70 languages
* The Anne Frank House museum

NOTEWORTHY

* Her diary is one of the most widely read books in the world
* Made into several films and plays
* There is also a *Book of Beautiful Sentences*

QUESTIONS

* What did Anne's father hope people would learn from her diary?
* Why did Anne and her family go into hiding?
* What is the name of the building in which they hid?
* Do you know of any other concentration camps?

Compare with Auschwitz, discrimination, Alexandra Zapruder, Holocaust, Adolf Hitler

Marie Curie

Marie Curie (born in 1867 in Poland, died in 1934 in France) was a Polish-French physicist and chemist. She is the only person to have won a Nobel Prize in both physics and chemistry.

Marie Skłodowska, as she was then known, moved to Paris after having been brought up in Warsaw. She studied physics and mathematics at the Sorbonne University. There she met her future husband, the physicist Pierre Curie. They were married in 1895 and had two daughters.

In 1896 the French physicist Henri Becquerel discovered that different uranium compounds give off a type of radiation that he called 'the radiation of uranium'. The following year, Marie Curie began studying this radiation that would later be called radioactivity. One year after that, she managed to isolate two highly radioactive elements. She named the first polonium – in reference to Poland, her country of origin – and the second, radium.

Pierre and Marie studied the characteristics of radiation. Among other discoveries, they found that radium emits heat and a radioactive gas (radon). They found that radiation could heal cancer and skin lesions, but also that it caused burns that were difficult to heal. In 1903, they were awarded the Nobel Prize in Physics, together with Becquerel. That same year Marie completed her doctoral thesis.

In 1906 Pierre Curie died after being run over by a horse-drawn waggon. Marie succeeded him as professor at the Sorbonne University, where she was the first woman to hold such a position. Previous-ly she had taught at a secondary school for young girls. Marie Curie continued to research radioactivity and in 1911 she received the Nobel Prize in Chemistry.

During the First World War, Marie Curie travelled with her daughter to the front. They examined wounded soldiers in ambulances that had been turned into mobile x-ray units. After the war she led the Institut du radium (Radium Institute) and focused in particular on the medical use of radium, called the Curie Therapy. The high doses of x-rays and radium radiation which Marie Curie was exposed to in her working environment probably caused the particular type of anaemia that finally cost her her life. She was unaware of the dangers of radiation and did not protect herself against it.

The eldest daughter of Marie and Pierre, Irène Joliot-Curie, received the Nobel Prize in Chemistry in 1935, together with her husband, Frédéric Joliot. Irène was also professor at the Sorbonne, head of the Institut du radium and for a short time, France's Undersecretary of State for Scientific Research in 1936. The youngest daughter of the Curies, Ève Curie, wrote a biography of her mother, titled *Madame Curie*.

In 1995 the remains of Marie and Pierre were moved to the Panthéon, a former church in Paris where distinguished French citizens are buried. The radioactive element curium was named after them. There is a Curie Museum in Paris and a Maria Skłodowska-Curie Museum in Warsaw. A bridge was also named after.

ne.se, britannica.com, Wikipedia.org

ALTERNATIVE CLUES

* The woman with two Nobel Prizes
* She was radio active
* Curious Curie

FACTS

* Born in Poland, died in France
* 1867-1934
* Moved to Paris to study
* Taught at a secondary school for young girls
* Discovered and named the elements polonium (after Poland) and radium
* Received the Nobel Prize in Physics in 1903, together with Pierre Curie and Henri Becquerel
* Received the Nobel Prize in Chemistry in 1911
* Is the only person to have received the prize in both physics and chemistry
* Examined and treated soldiers during the First World War
* Died from a disease probably caused by radioactive radiation

NOTEWORTHY

* Discovered radioactivity
* The first woman to receive a Nobel Prize
* The first woman professor at the Sorbonne
* The element curium is named after Marie and Pierre Curie
* Their daughter Irène Joliot-Curie also received a Nobel Prize (in Chemistry, 1935)

QUESTIONS

* In which country was Marie Curie born?
* What are the two elements she discovered?
* Which Nobel Prizes did she receive, and when?
* Nowadays men still receive more Nobel Prizes than women. Why?
* Marie Curie worked in a workshop without special anti-radiation protection. How would it be done nowadays?

Compare with Aletta Jacobs, Emma Leclercq, Alfred Nobel, Wilhelm Röntgen, Albert Einstein, Ada Lovelace, Chernobyl

23

Alfred Nobel

Alfred Nobel (1833-1896) was a Swedish chemist whose inventions include dynamite. He was very rich and determined that his wealth should be dedicated to things that were of use to humanity. This is how the Nobel Prizes for physics, chemistry, medicine, literature and peace came about.

Alfred Nobel's father, Immanuel Nobel, was an inventor. In 1838, he moved from Sweden to Saint Petersburg, because the Russian army was interested in the landmines he was making. The rest of the family followed four years later. Alfred learnt to speak Russian fluently and he was also proficient in English, German and French.

Following his studies in France and the United States, Alfred went to work at his father's workshop in Stockholm in 1863. There he looked for a method to safely use the explosive substance nitroglycerin. Nitroglycerin is an oily colourless liquid that is sensitive to shock, and therefore dangerous. In 1864 a violent explosion killed five people in the Nobel laboratory, including Alfred's brother Emil. As a result of the accident the production of nitroglycerin was banned in Stockholm. For a while, the laboratory was moved to a barge on a lake.

Alfred Nobel finally managed to stabilize nitroglycerin, by mixing it with earth made of fossilized algae. He called his invention dynamite (from the Greek *dynamis*, which means power). He also invented a detonator and a new explosive called gelignite, or blasting gelatin, that is not sensitive to water and is more powerful than dynamite. Finally, Alfred invented a practically smokeless powder explosive.

Nobel also dedicated himself to other types of inventions. He tried, for instance, to develop artificial silk and leather, but was not as successful. He ended up with a total of 355 patents to his name in various countries. This success formed the basis for a worldwide business empire. Nobel became a very wealthy man. In spite of this he lived a simple life. He never married and spent most of his time working, even in his villa in San Remo in Italy at the very end.

Alfred Nobel's brothers Robert and Louis also became wealthy, in particular from exploiting oil fields close to Baku, the capital of contemporary Azerbaijan. When Louis died in Cannes, a French journalist thought it was Alfred who had died. He wrote: 'The trader in death has died'.

Most of Alfred Nobel's inventions are indeed used in warfare, and a couple of years before his death he bought an arms manufacturing company. Alfred Nobel indicated in his will that the interest on his capital should be used to fund five Nobel Prizes per year, in physics, chemistry, medicine, literature and peace.

ne.se, britannica.org, wikipedia.org,nrc.nl, historiek.net

ALTERNATIVE CLUES

* Invented explosives but created a prize for peace
* The father of the world's most important prizes
* Celebrates a party every December 10

FACTS

* Inventor
* Initiator of the Nobel Prizes
* Born in Sweden, grew up in Russia, died in Italy
* 1833-1896
* His father invented landmines
* Invented dynamite
* Was a very wealthy businessman
* Was interested in peace

NOTEWORTHY

* Was shocked at being called 'The trader in death'
* His brothers were oil millionaires in Baku
* Left his money to fund the Nobel Prizes

QUESTIONS

* In which country close to Sweden did Alfred Nobel grow up?
* What were his most important inventions?
* How did he earn his money?
* Why was it so important for Alfred Nobel to be remembered as a man of peace?
* Who would you nominate for the Peace Prize, and why?
* Do you know any Nobel Prize winners?

Compare with Marie Curie, Albert Einstein, J. Robert Oppenheimer, Wilhelm Röntgen, arms trade

Ötzi

Ötzi, also called the Iceman, is the mummy of a man who lived more than 5,000 years ago. He was found in 1991, at a height of 3,210 metres on a glacier in Italy's South Tyrol, on the border to Austria. The mountains there are called the Ötztal Alps, which is why he was named Ötzi.

Ötzi was discovered by chance by two hikers. The hikers saw the body in a pool of melted snow under a rock. At first, they thought it was a tourist who had lost his or her way a few years earlier. This explains why the rescuers did not take special precautions when they tried to salvage the partly frozen body. They pulled and dragged at an arm and hacked away at the ice with an ice axe and a ski pole.

A couple of days later it became clear that this was a very special find indeed, of a man who had died a long time ago. He happened to have become visible because of the hot summer. A few days later he would have disappeared under the snow again.

Ötzi has been extensively examined. He lived about 5,300 years ago and was probably 45 years old when he died. He was 160 cm tall and weighed about 50 kg. Ötzi had dark, wavy hear, a beard, brown eyes and a big gap between his top front teeth. He had no caries, but his teeth were indeed worn down.

The mummified man had a broken nose and a couple of broken ribs, injuries that had later healed. The contents of his stomach revealed that his last meal consisted of meat and vegetables, and porridge or wheat bread. His body counted 61 tattoos, small cuts in the skin into which charcoal had been rubbed. They were probably the result of a therapeutic treatment such as acupuncture.

What is very special is that Ötzi's gear was also found, including a filled backpack. He wore a type of pants, a coat made of sheepskin, and a bear fur cap on his head. His leather shoes were lined with grass. He had a copper axe, copper being a desirable and valuable metal. The fact that Ötzi had such an axe shows that he held a high position in society. He also had a bow and arrows, a dagger and two cylindrical containers in which he probably kept charcoal embers to make fire.

An arrowhead in Ötzi's body shows that he was murdered. A deep cut in one of his hands suggests that he was involved in a fight shortly before his death. He also had a fractured skull from where he fell, or someone hit him on the head. Analyses of pollen in his stomach show that he died in June or July.

Ötzi was first kept in Austria. They later discovered that he had been found in Italy, 92.5 m from the border to Austria. The body is now in a museum in Bolzano, Italy, where it is kept in a cold chamber. You can look at Ötzi through a small window.

ALTERNATIVE CLUES

* An icy Italian
* Spent 5,000 years in a glacier
* Chilled mummy

FACTS

* Mummy from the Stone Age
* Italy
* Lived more than 5,000 years ago
* Named after the Ötztal Alps, where he was found by chance in 1991
* Remained frozen for 5,100 to 5,350 years
* Clothes and cap in bearskin
* His copper axe shows that he had a high status
* Was murdered – had an arrowhead in the body, a hand wound and a fractured skull
* Had 61 tattoos related to a therapeutic treatment
* About 45 years old, 160 cm tall, weighed 50 kg
* Can be seen in a museum in Italy

NOTEWORTHY

* A complete backpack was found beside him
* Had long dark hair, a beard, brown eyes and a gap between his front teeth
* A couple of his ribs are missing
* His nose was once broken
* Found in Italy, nearly 100 m from the border to Austria

QUESTIONS

* In what period did Ötzi live?
* Why is he called Ötzi?
* How did he die?
* When Ötzi was found in 1991, he was considered a very important find. Why?
* What have scientists learnt from this find?
* An arrowhead was found in his body. What do you think his final days were like?

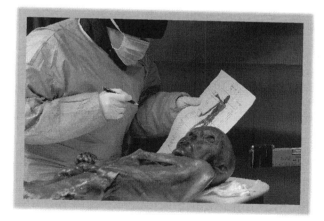

Compare with Cro-Magnon people, Lucy, Neanderthals, Peking Man, prehistory, Stonehenge

27

Rosa Parks

Rosa Parks (1913-2005) was a civil rights activist from the United States. She became famous for her act of resistance in 1955, when she refused to give up her seat in the bus for a white man.

Rosa Parks grew up in the state of Alabama in the South of the United States, where whites and blacks lived largely segregated. She worked as a seamstress in Montgomery, the capital of Alabama. She was active in the National Association for the Advancement of Colored People (NAACP), a civil rights organization.

On 1 December 1955, Rosa Parks was sitting in the rear part of a bus, formerly reserved for blacks. When all the seats for whites became occupied, the bus driver asked four blacks to stand. Rosa did not stand up. She refused.

Rosa Parks was arrested by the police and received a 14-dollar fine, which she refused to pay. Rosa Parks was not the first black person to refuse to give up their seat for a white, but local civil rights leaders decided to use her case in the struggle against racial segregation laws.

The southern states in particular experienced a long tradition of racial segregation following the abolition of slavery in 1865. In many areas, blacks had to use separate restaurants, public toilets and schools. There were even cities where black employees were essential during the day, but had to leave town before nightfall.

The decision to boycott the bus company was taken under the leadership of Reverend Martin Luther King. The campaign lasted more than a year, in spite of the fact that many participants were subjected to threats and accusations. Rosa Parks lost her job and the house of Martin Luther King was bombed. However, one year after the campaign started the Supreme Court ruled that segregation in public transport was unconstitutional and therefore illegal.

Rosa Parks contributed to this successful outcome by standing up for her rights. She became known throughout the country as 'the mother of the civil rights movement'. However, life in the South became too difficult for her and she and her husband moved to Detroit where she continued to fight for the rights of blacks.

Parks received many honours both during her life and after her death. Several songs have been written about her and she received the Presidential Medal of Freedom in 1996. She was one of the people invited to greet Nelson Mandela when he was freed from prison in South Africa in 1990.

When Rosa Parks died, she was the first woman to lie in honour in the Capitol, the congressional building in Washington. All flags were flown at half-staff on the day of her funeral, upon the order of President George W. Bush.

In 2014, an asteroid was named after Rosa Parks.

ne.se, britannica.com, wikipedia.org, CNN

ALTERNATIVE CLUES

* Refused to stand for whites
* She remained seated on a bus
* Inspired MLK

FACTS

* Civil rights activist
* US
* 1913-2005
* She grew up in segregation
* Was involved in the civil rights movement
* Was arrested and sentenced to pay a fine for not giving up her seat for a white man on the bus.
* Her action led to the bus boycott in Montgomery
* She worked together with Martin Luther King
* The Supreme Court found that segregation in busses was illegal
* She moved to Detroit and carried on with the struggle for black rights

NOTEWORTHY

* 'The mother of the civil rights movement'
* Greeted Nelson Mandela upon his liberation
* Lay in honour in the Capitol
* An asteroid was named after her

QUESTIONS

* In which part of the US did Rosa Parks grow up?
* What is she known for?
* What did she achieve with her action?
* Have you ever protested because you found something unfair?
* What would have happened if Rosa Parks had not protested?

Compare with Apartheid, civil rights movement, Malcolm X, Martin Luther King, Nelson Mandela, racial segregation, slavery

Mount Everest

At 8,848 metres, Mount Everest is the highest mountain in the world. It is located between Nepal and Tibet (China).

Mount Everest is a mountain in the Himalayas, a mountain range in South Asia. Its highest peak is situated 8,848 metres above sea level. Some scientists claim that the mountain is even two metres taller. To compare: The highest mountain in Western Europe is Mont Blanc at 4,808 metres.

Mount Everest was first charted by British surveyors in 1856. They named the mountain after the former head of British surveyors in India, Sir George Everest. The local population was naturally already acquainted with the mountain. The Tibetan name for the mountain is Chomolungma (Mother Goddess of the Earth). In Nepalese it is called Sagarmatha (Goddess of the Sky).

In the 1920s three British expeditions attempted to reach the summit of Mount Everest. As the North and South Poles had been conquered, the world's highest peak was one of the last places on earth where no one had ever set foot. George Mallory participated in all three expeditions. When asked why he wanted to climb Mount Everest, he said: 'Because it's there.' When Mallory and Andrew Irvine tried to reach the top in 1924, they disappeared. Mallory's body was only found in 1999. It is not clear whether they had reached the summit or not.

The first to have climbed to the top and to have returned alive were New-Zealander Edmund Hillary and the Nepalese Sherpa Tenzing Norgay. On 29 May 1953 they stood at the highest point on earth. Twenty-two years later, on 16 May 1975, Japan's Junko Tabei was the first woman to reach the summit. Since 1953, more than 6,000 people have climbed Mount Everest.

The youngest person to have climbed the mountain, Jordan Romero from the United States, was only 13 years old when he reached the top. On the occasion of the 2008 Olympic Games in Beijing, the Olympic torch was carried to the summit of Mount Everest.

It is very dangerous to climb Mount Everest. About five percent of mountaineers do not survive the attempt. The greatest risks are freezing conditions, exhaustion and a lack of oxygen. Due to this, climbers can easily make mistakes on their way back, which results in them falling or losing their way. Avalanches are another significant danger. The difficult conditions mean that it is practically impossible to help climbers in distress, or to bring bodies back down. Several dead mountaineers lay alongside the path.

It has become increasingly crowded on the mountain these past years. The weather is only good enough to reach the summit a few weeks per year, in May. Then the route sometimes carries a couple of hundred climbers.

ne.se, britannica.com, wikipedia.org

ALTERNATIVE CLUES

* Top spot
* Nearly nine kilometres high
* As high as it gets

FACTS

* A mountain in the Himalayas
* On the border of Nepal and Tibet (China)
* The highest mountain, 8,848 metres
* The British 1924 expedition failed
* New-Zealander Edmund Hillary and Sherpa Tenzing Norgay reached the summit in 1953
* In 1975 Japan's Junko Tabei was the first woman to climb to the top
* The climb is very dangerous and often claims lives

NOTEWORTHY

* Why do people climb the mountain? 'Because it's there,' said George Mallory
* Jordan Romero from the United States was only 13 years old when he reached the top
* It is a very dangerous climb

QUESTIONS

* Where is Mount Everest?
* What is the name of the mountain range that includes Mount Everest?
* Who was first to reach the summit?
* What exciting adventure would you like to experience?
* Why do people want to climb high mountains?

COMPARE WITH

Mariana Trench, K2, Mauna Kea

Easter Island

Easter Island is an island in the Pacific Ocean. It is part of Chile and lies 3,600 kilometres west of the mainland. Easter Island is especially known for its remarkable stone sculptures.

Easter Island is the easternmost island of Polynesia, a collective name for the islands and island groups of the Pacific Ocean. Easter Island is an island of volcanic origin. The majority of the population is Polynesian. Their ancestors probably arrived on Easter Island around 400 CE. The inhabitants of Easter Island are the only Polynesian people to have developed their own written language, now long extinct. This language – which resembles hieroglyphs – has still not been deciphered. This means that very little is known about the early history of the island.

Easter Island is very isolated. The closest inhabited island is more than 2,000 kilometres away. The first Europeans to visit Easter Island were from the Netherlands. An expedition looking for the legendary Great South Land arrived on the island on Easter Sunday 1722, which is how it got its name. During the second half of the nineteenth century, the population decreased dramatically, because of both newly imported diseases and the slave trade from Peru.

In 1888 the island was annexed by Chile. The Spanish name for the island is Isla de Pascua, which simply means Easter Island. In Polynesian it is called Rapa Nui. The island has about 4,800 inhabitants.

Easter Island is famous for its characteristic sculptures, called *moai*. There are a couple of hundred of them on the island. Most of the sculptures represent human shapes with a head and a trunk. As they are partly buried, often only the head is visible. The sculptures were made between 1100 and 1680 and were carved with simple tools out of huge blocks of volcanic stone. The sculptures were often placed on stone platforms.

The tallest statue to stand on a platform is 9.8 metres high and weighs about 74 tonnes. Some sculptures have a sort of stone headdress. The eye sockets originally housed white discs. According to one theory, these are statues of important people who had divine status. Another theory claims they are ancestors who look towards the skies and plead for fertility.

In the eighteenth and nineteenth centuries many of the sculptures were toppled or destroyed. There was probably internal fighting on the island. Meanwhile, dozens of sculptures have been restored.

Before Easter Island was inhabited, it was probably covered with forest. When the Europeans arrived, the only tree growing naturally on the island was a palm tree that only grew on Easter Island. The wood from the tree was very durable and the population used it amongst others to make canoes. When sheep were introduced on the island, the trees were gravely endangered. There was no wood left for canoes, which meant the inhabitants could no longer leave the island.

Easter Island has been listed by UNESCO as a World Heritage site since 1995.

ne.se, britannica.com, Wikipedia.org

ALTERNATIVE CLUES

* Moai
* Stone lifeguards on an isolated island

FACTS

* Island in the southeastern Pacific Ocean
* Belongs to Chile since 1888
* Inhabited since approximately 400 CE
* Was given its name by Dutch people who arrived on Easter Sunday 1722
* A very isolated island
* Especially known for its large stone statues made between 1100 and 1680
* Many of the statues are partly buried

NOTEWORTHY

* The statues probably plead for fertility
* Many of the statues were toppled
* Inhabitants created their own writing system that looks like hieroglyphs and has not yet been deciphered

QUESTIONS

* Where is Easter Island?
* Why is it called Easter Island?
* What is Easter Island most famous for?
* What must sailors have thought when they first saw the statues?
* Why do you think these statues were made?
* People on Easter Island had a form of writing that we have still not deciphered. Do you know other languages like that?

COMPARE WITH

Atlantis, Bermuda Triangle, Nazca Lines, Stonehenge, the pyramids

33

The pyramids of Giza

The pyramids of Giza are three huge tombs built approximately 4,500 years ago. They count amongst the largest surviving structures from antiquity.

The Egyptian city of Giza is situated on the western bank of the Nile River, 20 kilometres from the centre of the capital, Cairo. The two cities have now grown fully into each other. Just outside of Giza there are three huge pyramids named after the old Egyptian kings for whom they were built: Khufu, Khafre and Menkaure. They ruled during the 4th dynasty around 2575-2465 BCE. In the area around the three large pyramids, smaller pyramids were built for queens, together with a large number of graves for royal family members and paid workers.

The Pyramid of Khufu is the oldest and largest of the three main pyramids. It is 137 metres high (originally 147 metres) and its sides are 227 metres long at the base. It stands in an area the approximate size of five football fields. The pyramids of Khafre and Menkaure are respectively 136 metres and 62 metres high.

The pyramids were built of large blocks of limestone and granite. When the Pyramid of Khufu was completed, it was estimated to consist of 2.3 million blocks weighing an average of 2.5 tonnes each (about as much as two passenger cars). The stone blocks were positioned with impressive precision and skill. The corners of the pyramid point to the four cardinal directions.

It is not known how exactly the pyramids were built. According to the Greek historian Herodotus, who lived around 400 BCE, it took 20 years for 100,000 workers to build the Pyramid of Khufu.

Archaeological finds in the late twentieth century suggest about 20,000 men working throughout the year.

The pyramids were plundered long ago, both within and without. The contents of the tombs – the objects that accompanied the kings in their grave – have disappeared. Originally the pyramids were smooth on the outside because they were covered by a sort of cement of lime and sand. But this disappeared progressively, except from the top of the Pyramid of Khafre. Next to each pyramid there used to be a mortuary temple where the kings were worshipped.

The area was guarded by a colossal sphinx, a feline animal with the body of a lion and the face of a human. In ancient Egypt, the sphinx was a symbol of the king and god. The sphinx of Giza was carved into a limestone rock formation and is approximately 73 metres long and 20 metres high. The face is probably that of Khafre. The nose has disappeared.

King Khufu was the father and grandfather of Khafre and Menkaure. In fact, they were not pharaohs, although they often used that title. Pharaoh actually means 'great house' and was originally the name for a palace or courthouse. It is only in 1350 BCE, more than 1,000 years after Khufu's lifetime, that pharaoh was also used to designate the king himself.

The pyramids of Giza belong to the seven wonders of the ancient world. They are the only structures on the list that still exist. They are listed as a UNESCO World Heritage Site.

ALTERNATIVE CLUES

* Large houses for dead kings
* Stone upon stone upon stone upon...
* Largest tombs in the world
* The guard has lost its nose

FACTS

* Huge old tombs
* Egypt
* Built about 4,500 years ago
* The pyramids were built for the kings Khufu, Khafre and Menkaure
* The Pyramid of Khufu is the oldest and largest, 137 metres high
* The pyramids consist of millions of blocks of limestone and granite
* The contents of the tombs were stolen by plunderers
* The area is guarded by a giant sphinx

NOTEWORTHY

* The approximate 2.3 million stone blocks of the Pyramid of Khufu weigh about 2,500 kg each
* We still do not know exactly how the Egyptians built the pyramids
* The nose of the sphinx has disappeared
* The Pyramid of Khufu was the tallest building in the world for 4,000 years

QUESTIONS

* In which country are the pyramids of Giza?
* What are the pyramids?
* For which king was the largest pyramid built?
* Which other famous tombs or funerary monuments do you know? Where are they situated?

COMPARE WITH

Cleopatra, the Nile, Ötzi, sphinx, Stonehenge, Taj Mahal, Tutankhamun

The Terracotta Army

The Terracotta Army consists of approximately 8,000 clay (terracotta) sculptures that were found by chance. The figures, are more than 2,000 years old, guard the mausoleum of the first emperor of China.

Three Chinese farmers came across a strange find when they started to dig a well to pump water in 1974. In the ground, they saw pieces of pottery made of red baked clay, *terracotta*. When they dug further, they found a full statue of a soldier. Archaeologists came to take a look and carried on digging. All in all, they found 8,000 figures that are 2,200 years old.

The Terracotta Army guards the enormous burial mound of the first emperor of China. The sculptures are life size. The army consists of cavalry warriors and charioteers with horses and chariots, as well as infantry warriors and archers. The warriors are thought to represent real life people. Every warrior has their own facial features and researchers have discovered that their ears also vary from one figure to the other.

The weapons were still sharp after all this time. Originally, the images were painted with bright colours, but these have since faded. Statues of officials, acrobats and musicians were also found among the warriors.

Emperor Qin Shi Huang was the first emperor of China. He lived from 259 to 210 BCE. Qin Shi Huang was a stern leader. He had succeeded his father as ruler of Qin State, in the north of today's China.

Through a combination of diplomatic and military conquests, he managed to unite a number of Chinese states. This is why he is considered the first emperor of China.

Shi Huang carried out a number of important reforms. He standardized the currency, the writing system, and weights and measures. To protect the empire against enemies he laid the basis for the Great Wall of China.

The construction of Qin Shi Huang's huge tomb started during his lifetime. Qin Shi Huang believed that it was his palace for eternity and that life underground would be a continuation of life aboveground. His tomb is surrounded by burial chambers with gifts that were intended to feed and protect his soul in the afterlife. Only a few of the close to 100 burial chambers have been opened as of yet. Countless treasures remain underground. There are concerns that opening the tomb may damage precious objects beyond repair. It is also unclear where the entrance lies.

It is said that upon completion of the tomb, those who worked on its construction were buried alive in the underground complex, to prevent them from sharing the secrets of the palace.

Later, the Terracotta Army was gradually covered with a three-metre thick layer of sand. This is how the army came to lie underground for 2,200 years. Qin Shi Huang's Mausoleum is inscribed on UNESCO's World Heritage List. The associated museum attracts millions of visitors every year.

wikipedia.org

ALTERNATIVE CLUES

* Immortalized stone soldiers
* 8,000 protective men made of clay
* Harmless Chinese army

FACTS

* 8,000 sculptures close to the tomb of a Chinese emperor
* China
* Completed around 210 BCE
* Discovered in 1974, as farmers were looking for water
* Approximately 8,000 soldiers and horses
* Also acrobats and musicians
* The tomb itself is an underground palace that has yet to be excavated

NOTEWORTHY

* Every soldier has their own facial features
* The weapons that were found were still sharp
* All those who worked on the tomb were probably buried alive

QUESTIONS

* What is the Terracotta Army?
* Where is the Terracotta Army?
* Why did the emperor have the army built?
* Why has the burial complex not been excavated in full?
* Do you know any other special mausoleums?

COMPARE WITH

The Great Wall of China, the Giza Pyramids, Easter Island, the Forbidden City in Beijing

Braille

Braille is a font that can be read with your fingertips. It was developed for people who are blind and visually impaired by Louis Braille, who was himself blind.

Louis Braille was a Frenchman who lived from 1809 to 1852. When he was three years old he poked himself in the eye with an awl. He became blind in that eye and developed an infection that also caused blindness in the other eye. In 1818 he went to Paris to study at one of the first schools for blind children in the world. From 1826 he was himself a teacher at the school.

Braille first thought of his system when he attended a school presentation by an army captain who had developed 'night writing' for Napoleon. The idea was for soldiers to be able to receive communications on the battlefield, silently and without light. The system consisted of a matrix of six dots by two pricked into a sheet of paper from behind.

This system did not succeed because it was too difficult to read. However, 11-year-old Louis Braille was very enthusiastic. He refined the technique and reduced the number of dots to a matrix of three by two that seemed more workable.

He made the entire alphabet using each time a maximum of six dots. Together with a few simple aids, this makes it possible for the blind and visually impaired to read and also write. The Braille method was only recognized as an official alphabet after Louis' death. It then spread all over the world.

Braille is a so-called tactile alphabet. Blind persons feel the embossed dots with their fingertips. A drawback of the embossing is that it makes books very thick. One of the solutions for this is to use contractions. Nowadays, the blind and visually impaired can read braille on a laptop, by adding a braille reading line, or reader. This device produces the proper tactile characters with a matrix consisting of dots.

In 1845 the British national William Moon developed an alternative tactile alphabet, based on the shape of regular letters. The Moon alphabet is easier to learn for people who can already read and become blind later in life. It is less common than braille but is also still used.

ALTERNATIVE CLUES

* Finger-top feeling
* Reading by feeling
* With these dots you can read without looking

FACTS

* Writing that you read with your fingertips
* The characters are pressed into the paper
* Developed by Louis Braille, a Frenchman. Lived from 1809 to 1852
* Louis Braille was 11 years old and blind when he developed the system
* It consists of characters with a maximum of six dots
* Braille can be read by people who are blind or visually impaired
* Moon writing is an alternative to braille

NOTEWORTHY

* Louis Braille developed braille when he was 11 years old
* Braille can also be read with a laptop
* Books in braille are very thick

QUESTIONS

* What is braille?
* What are braille characters made of?
* How can you read braille with a computer?
* What other ways do you know of communicating with letters?

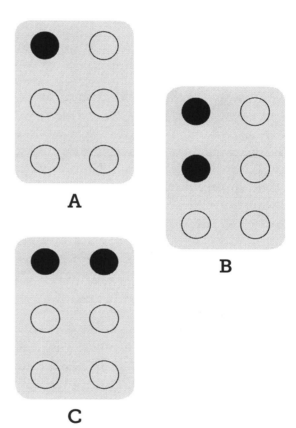

A

B

C

COMPARE WITH

Esperanto, hieroglyphs, Morse, the five senses

The Titanic

The Titanic was a huge passenger ship that sank on its maiden journey; 1,522 people drowned.

In 1912, when the Titanic left the shipyard in Belfast, it was the largest ship in the world. Titanic means gigantic and is derived from the Titans of Greek mythology. The ship was 269 metres long, 28 metres wide and 53 metres tall from the keel to the top of the chimney. It had four chimneys, the fourth of which was only added because it looked better. The ship was intended to sail over the Atlantic Ocean, back and forth between Great Britain and the United States.

The interior was very luxurious. The first class had four lifts, a large dining hall, a library and a swimming pool. The third class was also comfortable when compared with other ships. Because of a system of fully automatic doors between the compartments, the Titanic was thought to be unsinkable.

On 10 April 1912, the Titanic left the port of Southampton. After picking up passengers in France and Ireland, the ship continued its voyage westward with New York as its final destination. There were about 2,200 people on board, including 1,300 passengers.

On 14 April at 23:40 hours, a sailor on the lookout saw an iceberg ahead. It was too late to avoid it. The Titanic collided with the iceberg. Holes appeared in the hull and water began to stream in. The ship's designer Thomas Andrews, who was on board, rapidly concluded that the ship that was considered unsinkable would indeed sink.

Captain Edward Smith ordered distress signals to be sent. At his request, the ship's band continued to play on the deck to prevent panic from breaking out.

The lifeboats only had enough capacity for about half of the passengers. Many of these boats were also lowered with too few passengers on board. Not to mention that many people were not aware of the seriousness of the situation. The heaviest loss of life was among the crew and third class passengers.

When the bow began to sink, the stern was lifted out of the water, causing the ship to break in two. At 2:20 a.m. the stern also disappeared under water. People who ended up in the water drowned or died from the cold. Ships that heard the distress signal arrived too late and were only able to rescue people in the lifeboats. A total of 1,522 people lost their life.

Two years after the disaster, an even larger sister ship of the Titanic, the Britannic, was put to water. Its design had been changed to prevent it from sinking. However, that ship also sank, in 1916. It was hit by a naval mine or a torpedo attack in the Aegean Sea.

In 1985 the wreck of the Titanic was found at the bottom of the ocean at a depth of 3,800 metres.

wikipedia.org

ALTERNATIVE CLUES

* A devastating iceberg
* A giant at the bottom of the ocean
* Tragic maiden voyage

FACTS

* A ship
* Great-Britain
* Sank during its maiden voyage in 1912
* The largest ship in the world
* The Titanic was 260 metres long and had very luxurious fittings
* It collided with an iceberg around midnight
* There were not enough lifeboats and too few people in each boat
* More than 1,500 of the 2,200 people on board died
* The wreck was found in 1985 at a depth of 3,810 metres

NOTEWORTHY

* The Titanic was at that time the largest ship in the world
* The ship was thought to be unsinkable
* The band kept on playing while the ship sank

QUESTIONS

* Between which cities was the Titanic set to sail?
* Why did the ship sink?
* Why did so few people survive the disaster?
* How do ships detect icebergs nowadays?

COMPARE WITH

SOS signal, Titans, Morse code, icebergs

Apollo 11

Apollo 11 was the space mission that took the first humans to the Moon. Astronaut Neil Armstrong set foot on the Moon on 21 July 1969.

The Apollo project was an American space project aimed at landing people on the Moon. It was named after the Greek god Apollo. The project lasted from 1961 to 1972. It began shortly after the Soviet cosmonaut Yuri Gagarin carried out the first human spaceflight on 12 April 1961.

The space race between the United States and the Soviet Union was fully underway. US President John F. Kennedy wanted to restore the superiority of the United States in the area of technology. "We choose to go to the moon, not because it is easy, butbecause it is hard".

The successful Apollo 11 mission was preceded by ten tests. The first was disastrous: three astronauts died in an exercise when fire broke out in the space capsule. This was followed by a series of tests with a Saturn rocket and unmanned spacecraft. Apollo 7 was the first human spaceflight to circle the Earth. Then came successful unmanned moon landings.

On 16 July 1969, Neil Armstrong, Michael Collins and Edwin 'Buzz' Aldrin left the Earth. Apollo's rocket was called Saturn V. The spacecraft flew 1.5 times around the Earth before setting course for the Moon, 380,000 kilometres away.

Armstrong and Aldrin uncoupled the Eagle lunar module from the Columbia mothership, in which Collins continued to circle the Moon. On 21 July the Eagle landed on the Moon. The astronauts were in dire need of sleep, but did not want to wait any longer. Armstrong climbed out of the lander, and when he first set foot on the Moon, he said: 'One small step for man, one giant leap for mankind.'

Armstrong and Aldrin remained outside for two and a half hours. They planted the American flag, took photographs and collected about twenty kilogrammes of samples from the surface of the moon. Armstrong spoke with President Nixon on the telephone. Films show them jumping around in their large spacesuits. Then they returned to the mothership and arrived back on Earth three days later. Only years later did the astronauts admit that the American flag was blown over by the rocket engine immediately upon take-off.

The Americans returned six times to the Moon after this. Apollo 13 had to return after having circled the Moon once, due to damage caused at launch. A total of twelve astronauts have been on the Moon. The last three missions also included an electrical car with which astronauts drove around dozens of kilometres.

ne.se, wikipedia.org, nasa.gov

ALTERNATIVE CLUES

* The Eagle has landed
* The space rece winner
* The first foot on a far off stone

FACTS

* The first person on the Moon
* US
* 16-24 July 1969
* The Apollo project aimed to bring humans to the Moon
* Apollo 11 left Earth on 16 July 1969
* The crew consisted of Neil Armstrong, Michael Collins and Edwin 'Buzz' Aldrin
* The lunar module was called the Eagle
* Armstrong took the first step on the surface of the moon
* Aldrin and Armstrong stayed 2.5 hours outside
* They took 20 kilogrammes of stone with them back to earth

NOTEWORTHY

* 'One small step for man, one giant leap for mankind'
* Armstrong and Aldrin planted a US flag on the moon, but the rocket engine blew it over
* It was a space race between the US and the Soviet Union

QUESTIONS

* In what year did the Apollo 11 expedition take place?
* Who was the first human on the Moon?
* What was the name of the lunar lander?
* The voyages to the Moon and the space race were extremely expensive projects. Do you see a point in spending a lot of money on this?
* Do you think there will be more human voyages to the Moon?

COMPARE WITH

Yuri Gagarin, Cold War, Laika, discovery journeys, Valentina Tereshkova

Blue whales

The blue whale is the largest animal in the world. It is a whale that eats small krill.

Blue whales can grow to be more than 30 metres long. That is longer than two trucks with trailers. Large specimens weigh 150,000 kilogrammes. To compare: That is 15 times the weight of a large elephant.

Blue whales are dark blue-grey with light patches. Blue whales are baleen whales. They have baleen plates instead of teeth. The plates are comb-like filters that hang from their top jaw. They use them to filter small sea animals from the water.

Blue whales feed from small crustaceans called krill. They take in water and push it out again through the baleens, leaving the krill behind.

The eyes of blue whales are small. They do not see very well. Their sense of smell is probably not very well developed either, although they do have good hearing. They communicate using low-frequency sounds that can be heard 200 kilometres away.

Blue whales have blowholes on their head. They use them to breathe. This occurs with great speed and force. When they breathe out, a column of water is created that can reach up to 10 metres. They sleep while drifting on the surface of the water.

There are blue whales in all oceans. In the summer, they look for food in the North Pole area, where there are much plankton. They spend the rest of the year in warmer waters around the equator, where they reproduce. These animals are very difficult to study as they swim at great depths and travel a lot.

Whales are mammals who nurse their calves. Females have a calf every one to two years. They are pregnant for one year at most. New-born calves are seven to eight metres long and weigh approximately 2,700 kilogrammes. They drink around 200 litres of milk per day and remain at least six months with their mother so they can continue to nurse.

In spite of their huge mass, blue whales are capable of jumping fully out of the water. They are indeed known for their acrobatic jumps.

This enormous animal has no natural enemies, except for humans. From the late nineteenth century to the mid-twentieth century, hundreds of thousands of whales were killed for their meat and also for their blubber, which was used to make lamp oil. Since 1966, blue whales have been protected and their numbers have increased. However, the animal species is still extremely endangered by illegal hunting and the pollution of the oceans.

wikipedia.org

ALTERNATIVE CLUES

* This animal is 15 times heavier than an elephant
* XXXXXL marine mammal
* Blue giant of the oceans

FACTS

* Baleen whale
* More than 30 metres long
* 150,000 kilogrammes
* Can be found in all oceans
* Dark blue-grey with light patches
* They catch their food with baleens, a type of filter
* Feed on small crustaceans
* Spend the summer in the North Pole area
* Hundreds of thousands have been killed since the 19th century
* They are protected since 1966, but remain threatened

NOTEWORTHY

* The largest animal on earth
* A new-born calf is eight metres long, weighs 2,700 kg and drinks 200 litres of milk per day
* Make sounds that can be heard 200 kilometres away
* Can spray water columns as tall as a house

QUESTIONS

* What do blue whales eat and how do they catch their food?
* What type of animal would you like to see in real life? Why?
* What threatens blue whales?

COMPARE WITH

Dinosaurs, sharks, octopuses, mammals

Dinosaurs

Dinosaurs are reptiles that became extinct 66 million years ago. They were often very large and voracious.

No human being has ever seen one alive, although they do excite the imagination: dinosaurs. These reptiles lived from 252 to 66 million years ago. Our knowledge of dinosaurs is based on fossils. Fossils are the petrified remains of bones, footprints, eggs and faeces.

The first dinosaurs were rather small and often fast-moving creatures that walked on their hind legs. The earliest-known dinosaur is called Eoraptor. It was about as large as a cat and ate both plants and meat.

The most famous dinosaurs are the enormous predators like Tyrannosaurus Rex that reached up to 12 metres in length and weighed about as much as an elephant. They had huge jaws and teeth that could even crush bones. The largest predatory dinosaur was probably the Spinosaurus that was up to 15 metres long.

Sauropods were the largest creatures ever to walk the earth at that time. The Diplodocus is an example of these. Contrary to predatory dinosaurs that walked on their hind legs, Sauropods were four-legged animals that ate plants. They had long necks and tails and lived in herds. The largest specimens are thought to have reached 40 metres and weighed up to 100,000 kilogrammes. Some dinosaurs swallowed stones that helped grind the food in their stomach.

Many herbivorous dinosaurs developed all types of armour against predatory dinosaurs. Some had plates of bone on their neck, shoulders and back. Rhinoceroses such as the Triceratops had a wide shield on their back. Other animals also armed themselves against voracious predators. Nocturnal animals, like certain types of squirrels, probably appeared during this period. During the day, they hid from dinosaurs.

There were also flying dinosaurs, the precursors of birds. Birds are in fact the only surviving dinosaurs.

For a long time scientists debated what caused dinosaurs to become extinct 66 million years ago. Currently, most agree that it was probably an enormous meteorite striking of what is now Mexico. The impact released a lot of lava from under the ground. Temperatures rose and fire broke out everywhere. Many animals died instantly. Others did not survive because there was so much soot and dust in the air that sunlight was unable to reach the ground for years.

People have invented the 'cosmic calendar' to get an impression of the period in which dinosaurs lived. On this calendar, the age of the earth is reduced to one year. The big bang occurred at midnight on 1 January. The first dinosaurs appeared on 25 December, the first flowers on 27 December and the first apes on 30 December. That day, dinosaurs became extinct. At 10:30 p.m. on 31 December, the first species of humans appeared. The history of modern humans plays itself out in the last 10 seconds of the year. The Middle Ages end about one second ago.

ALTERNATIVE CLUES

* Extinct giants
* You can't find these animals in a park

FACTS

* Large reptiles
* Lived 230 to 66 million years ago
* Tyrannosaurus Rex was a 12-metre long predator
* Diplodocus could reach 40 metres in length, the largest land animal
* They often had armour
* They became extinct following a meteorite impact
* Our knowledge of dinosaurs is based on fossils

NOTEWORTHY

* Birds are dinosaurs
* Some swallowed stones to grind the food in their stomach
* Certain animal species started their day at night so as not to be eaten

QUESTIONS

* When did dinosaurs become extinct, and what caused it?
* The largest dinosaur was 40-metres long. Would it fit in your classroom?
* What is a fossil?
* Dinosaurs became extinct a long time ago. Imagine scientists finding us in 10,000 years. What would surprise them most?

Brachiosaurus

Velociraptor

Elasmosaurus

COMPARE WITH

Fossils, Jurassic Park, cosmic calendar, Chicxulub crater

47

Chess

Chess is a game played with 32 pieces on a square board made up of 64 squares. The winner is the person who succeeds in taking the king of their opponent.

Each of the two chess players has six different types of pieces that move differently over the board: one king, one queen, two knights, two bishops, two rooks and eight pawns. White begins. The players take turns making a move.

Pawns can only move forward, which means they can never move back to a previous position. Rooks can move one or more squares forward, backward, or sideward. Bishops can only move diagonally. Knights make strange jumps: two steps forward and one step sideward. The queen can move like a rook or a bishop. It is the most powerful piece on the chessboard. The king can only move one square.

The objective of the game is to checkmate (or in short, to mate) the king of your opponent. When the king is threatened with capture, it is in check. If it cannot repel the attack, it is mated, and the opponent has won. A chess game can also end in a stalemate – or draw – if no further moves are possible, or if both players agree on a draw.

Chess playing rules are rather easy to learn, but it is difficult to become very good at the game. The pieces have to work well together, you have to attack and defend at the same time, and you have a huge choice of possible moves. 'If I do this, my opponent will probably do that. And then, I can best respond with this.' You often see chess players think for a long time before they make their move.

At chess tournaments players use a clock. Each player may for instance spend one hour on their first 40 moves. Once you have made a move, you turn off your clock and turn on the clock of your opponent. You can also play rapid chess, in which games are decided in five minutes, for instance.

Simultaneous exhibitions are a special type of chess playing in which one experienced player plays against multiple opponents at once – usually about 20 of them. The player walks from one table to the next, making one rapid move each time. The world record is held by the Iranian Ehsan Ghaem-Maghami, who played against 604 opponents. He won 580 games, had 16 draws and eight losses.

Chess is thought to be a very old game. It has probably been played for thousands of years. It is played all over the world and the best players are professionals. Most world champions are from the Soviet Union and later Russia, including Anatoly Karpov and Garry Kasparov. One of the most talented players was Bobby Fischer, from the United States. Hungary's Judit Polgár is the best female chess player.

For a long time, computer programmers worked on a chess computer that could beat top players. This finally succeeded in 1997, when the Deep Blue computer beat world champion Kasparov.

ne.se, brittannica.com, Wikipedia.org

ALTERNATIVE CLUES

* 64 white or black squares
* Mate!
* With a mighty queen

FACTS

* A board game with 64 squares and 32 pieces
* Thousands of years old
* Every player has a king, a queen, two knights, two bishops, two rooks and eight pawns
* White begins
* The objective is to checkmate the king of your opponent
* You can also reach a stalemate or draw

NOTEWORTHY

* The trick is to think far ahead
* In 1997 the Deep Blue computer beat a world champion for the first time
* Ehsan Ghaem-Maghami played simultaneously against 604 opponents and won 580 games

QUESTIONS

* What is the objective in chess?
* What are the different pieces called?
* What is the strongest piece?
* Does it seem like a fun game? Why?

COMPARE WITH

Backgammon, Go, Bobby Fischer, Kasparov, Judit Polgár

Notes

Sources

Sources of the pictures in this book:

Cover: Shutterstock / South Tyrol Museum of Archeology
Back cover: Erik Saanila, Pelaago Photography
Introduction: Shutterstock, Ela Strandberg

1.   The Nobel Foundation
2.   Collection Anne Frank House, Amsterdam
3.   Nasa
4.   Shutterstock
5.   Shutterstock
6.   Wikimedia, Pixabay
7.   Wikimedia
8.   Wikimedia
9.   Shutterstock
10. Pixabay, Project Possible
11. South Tyrol Museum of Archeology
12. Shutterstock
13. Wikimedia
14. Wikimedia
15. Wikimedia

Would you like to find out more about Grej of the Day?

Or get further details on how to apply it in your classroom? Would you like the rest of your team to become acquainted with it?

Invite Micael Hermansson to give a presentation.
Micael is an experienced presenter and one of Scandinavia's top speakers. He will tell you the inspiring story of how it all started and why and how the concept works. Suitable for all group sizes.
More info: micaelhermansson.com
Join the Facebook group Grej of the Day (International).
To exchange ideas and lessons with colleagues. More information at www.grejoftheday.com

Made in the USA
Monee, IL
15 January 2023

25353009R00031